Maine

Titanic

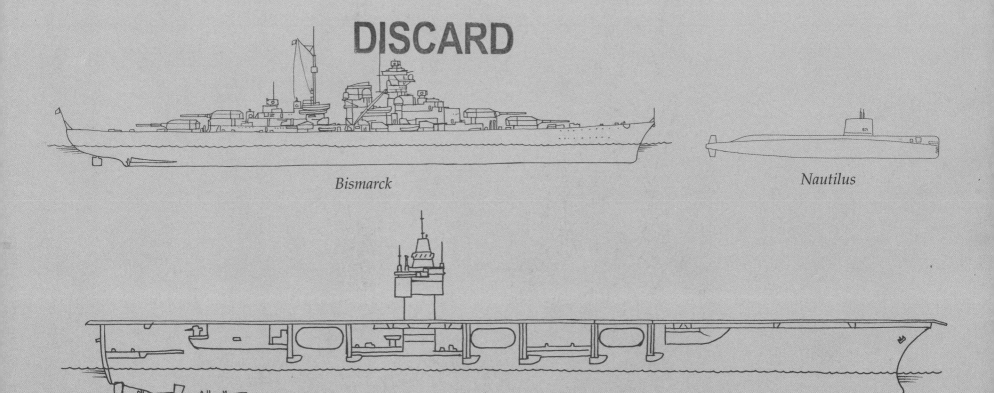

Bismarck

Nautilus

Enterprise

The Great Ships

Patrick O'Brien

Walker & Company ✺ New York

Old sailors know that every ship on the sea has its own personality. Some ships seem to skip along the waves, but others creak and roll as they labor through the seas. When a sailor talks about his ship, he will say "she" instead of "it," as in "She's a greasy old ship but she sails well." Each ship is thought of as an individual and so, unlike cars, trains, or most airplanes, ships are given proper names.

The earliest ships whose names stand out in history were three small Spanish caravels that set sail in 1492. There was nothing out of the ordinary about the *Niña*, the *Pinta*, and the *Santa Maria* when Columbus sailed them on his voyage of discovery to the New World. But the three names are forever remembered for the part they played in making history.

Since that time, many ships have made the history books. Most are famous because they have been a part of great events of the past. Others have become famous because of their captains. Some are even best known for their disastrous ends.

In the swift longships of the Vikings and the massive aircraft carriers of today, in humble little caravels and mighty men-of-war, sailors have gone to sea with the urge to roam, to explore, to conquer. It is this spirit of adventure and exploration that has made the great ships great.

The Gokstad Ship

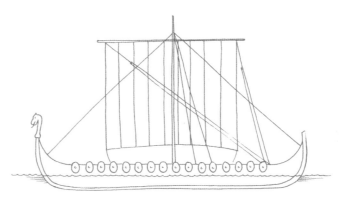

A thousand years ago, Vikings sailed the seas. The Vikings were a fierce and adventurous people who lived in the rugged lands of Scandinavia in northern Europe. They built ships called longships that were strong enough to weather storms at sea but light enough to be sailed right up onto a beach or rowed along shallow rivers. Other sailors of that time sailed only along the coastlines for fear of getting lost, but the Vikings weren't afraid to take their rugged ships out into the open ocean, where no land was in sight. A Viking captain named Leif Eriksson sailed west from his home in Greenland and discovered North America five hundred years before Columbus.

The Vikings sailed their longships along the coasts of Europe, attacking and robbing churches, towns, and cities. Some of the Vikings stayed behind in France and the British Isles. They built villages and started farms, and over the years intermingled with the people already living there. To this day, there is still some Viking blood in the British and French people.

In 1880 near Gokstad, Norway, something surprising was dug from the grave of a Viking chieftain. It was a longship, and it had lain in the earth for a thousand years. The Vikings buried it along with their dead leader so that even after death, he could go on sailing the seas in his longship.

Even after a thousand years underground, most of the ship was still in good shape.

5

Cheng Ho's Treasure Ship

The Chinese have been sailing Asian waters for a thousand years or more in ships called "junks." The word *junk* comes from an old Malaysian word *jong*. The hull of a junk is built like a large, flat-bottomed box. It is divided inside by watertight wooden walls so that if the junk were to spring a leak, only one area of the hull would fill with water and the junk would not sink.

Probably the biggest junk, and one of the biggest wooden ships ever built anywhere in the world, was the "treasure ship" of Admiral Cheng Ho. It was four hundred feet long, almost four times longer than Christopher Columbus's largest ship eighty-seven years later. From the decks of this enormous junk Cheng Ho commanded a fleet of more than three hundred ships and twenty-seven thousand men. The Chinese emperor had assembled the fleet to demonstrate to other countries how rich and powerful he was. From 1405 to 1433, Cheng Ho sailed on seven long expeditions throughout the South China Sea and the Indian Ocean, visiting the coasts of India, Arabia, and Africa.

Junks were much better sailing ships than the small vessels of the early European explorers in the 1400s. But the Chinese junk remained unchanged for hundreds of years after that, while shipbuilders in Europe continually improved their craft. When the Chinese emperor decided to stop all foreign voyages in 1433, the seas were left to the adventurous Europeans to explore in their little wooden ships.

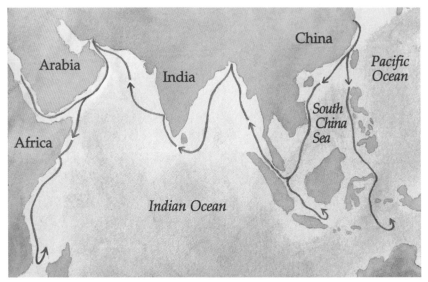

No one is sure of the exact routes, but this map shows the area covered by Cheng Ho's voyages.

The Niña, the Pinta, & the Santa Maria

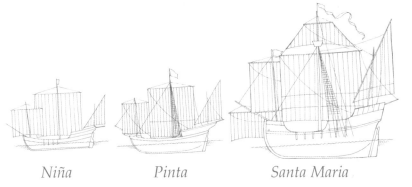

Niña   *Pinta*   *Santa Maria*

The *Niña*, the *Pinta*, and the *Santa Maria* made what could be the most important sea voyage in history. The discovery of the New World opened the age of European exploration and changed the world forever.

These three ships were a common type of Spanish ship called a "caravel." They were very small and offered the captain and crew almost no shelter from the weather. There were no sleeping quarters for the crew, so at night the sailors just tried to find a comfortable spot on the deck or amid the baggage. But these little wooden ships were sturdy and reliable, and in them the Spanish began to explore the world.

In 1492 the *Niña*, the *Pinta*, and the *Santa Maria* sailed from Spain under the command of Christopher Columbus. He was looking for a route to China and Japan, then called the Far East. Since the world is round, he was confident that he could get to the East by sailing west. What he didn't know was that the Americas were in the way.

After weeks of sailing west from Spain with the wind behind them, the sailors began to wonder how they would ever get back home. On October 10, Columbus told his men that if no land was found in three days they would turn back. Two days later, the lookout cried, "Land! Land!"

Columbus had accidentally found a tiny island in the Caribbean, but thought that he had found the islands of the Far East. To his dying day he remained convinced that Japan was just over the horizon instead of half a world away.

The Santa Maria *made only a one-way trip to the Americas. She was wrecked on a reef before she could return to Spain. Columbus and his crew crowded into the* Niña *and the* Pinta *for the trip home.*

The Golden Hind

Sir Francis Drake was an English ship captain who attacked and robbed Spanish treasure ships. The Spanish called him a pirate, but the English called him a hero. He brought fortunes in gold back to England, which he presented to the queen, Elizabeth I.

The Spanish were taking huge amounts of gold and jewels from their colonies in Central and South America, and sending the wealth back to Spain on giant treasure ships called "galleons." The galleons were well armed with big cannons to keep away any ships that might want to rob them of their treasure. But the Spanish did not guard their colonies and ships on the Pacific coast of the Americas. They did not expect foreign ships to be so far from Europe. And they did not expect Drake's daring plan.

In 1577 Drake set out from England in the *Golden Hind* on a mission to capture Spanish gold. He sailed across the Atlantic and all the way around Cape Horn, at the southern tip of South America, and into the Pacific Ocean. There the Spanish assumed that the *Golden Hind* was a Spanish vessel, so Drake was able to sail up to unsuspecting ships without a fight. Then Drake's men would suddenly attack. They even at-tacked small Spanish towns along the Pacific coast of South America. When he had filled the *Golden Hind*'s hold with gold and jewels, it was time to return to England.

The Spanish were waiting for Drake at Cape Horn. They expected that he would return there on his way back home, and they would take their treasure back. But Drake had a surprise for them. He sailed west, crossed the Pacific, and traveled all the way around the world to get back to England. It was a very long and hazardous trip, but nearly three years after leaving home, Drake sailed triumphantly back into the harbor at Plymouth, England. The *Golden Hind* was only the second ship ever to sail around the world, and Drake was the first captain ever to make the entire trip.

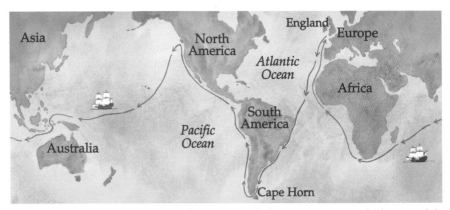

This map shows Drake's route around the world.

The Mayflower

We don't really know what the *Mayflower* looked like. No one thought to paint or draw any pictures of her in her time. She was just an ordinary ship that was hired to take a group of immigrants, the Pilgrims, to their new lives in America.

The Pilgrims were a group of people that were unhappy with their home country of England. They were not allowed to practice their religion as they wanted, so they decided to pack up and move to the new colonies in America. They hired a ship and a captain, and set off across the Atlantic Ocean.

The crossing was not easy. Most of the time the passengers on the *Mayflower* were cold, wet, and seasick. There wasn't quite enough food on board, and by the time they reached America they were half starved. Then their real troubles began.

When the Pilgrims landed in Massachusetts at the beginning of the winter of 1620, they didn't know how to make a living in the cold, rocky wilderness. During that first hard winter nearly half of them died of disease or just from the cold. But the next spring, when the captain of the *Mayflower* sailed home to England, all of the surviving Pilgrims chose to stay behind and make a new life in the New World.

The Mayflower reached America at Cape Cod in Massachusetts. From there the Pilgrims explored the coastline for a good place to start their colony. They chose Plymouth Bay.

The Queen Anne's Revenge

Blackbeard the pirate was a mean and dangerous man. He was so terrifying to look at that a lot of his victims gave up without a fight. He was very tall with fierce, dark eyes. He had a big black beard that he tied into small tails with colored ribbons. When on the attack, he wore a leather band across his chest with three pistols hanging from it. But the crowning touch was the burning fuses he shoved under his hat, so that his snarling face was surrounded by smoke and fire.

In 1717 Blackbeard captured a French ship, put extra cannons on board, and renamed her the *Queen Anne's Revenge*. Then he and his pirates went raiding, attacking weaker ships in the Caribbean Sea and along the southeastern coast of the American colonies. Usually he would steal the money, gold, and jewels on board, but sometimes he would take the whole ship. Soon he had captured more ships than he needed, and he decided that he didn't want the *Queen Anne's Revenge* anymore. He had his pirates take everything he wanted off the ship, and then they beached it on a sandbar. Blackbeard sailed away in another ship, leaving the *Queen Anne's Revenge* to gradually break up in the wind and waves.

"Blackbeard" was a nickname. The fearsome pirate's real name was Edward Teach.

The *Bounty*

The island of Tahiti in the South Pacific Ocean was a paradise on Earth. It had tall green mountains with clear running streams and long sandy beaches shaded by palm trees. When the trading ship *Bounty* arrived there in 1789, the friendly islanders paddled out to welcome the weary sailors to their island with food and gifts.

The sailors of the *Bounty* had just spent sixteen difficult months on board the ship sailing from England. They ate the same bad food every day and lived in the crowded, dirty areas below deck. If they broke one of the many rules, the captain, William Bligh, made sure that punishment was swift and harsh.

When the *Bounty* set out from Tahiti to return to England, some of the sailors decided they wanted to go back to the island paradise. One dark night they burst into Captain Bligh's cabin with guns drawn and swords ready. This was mutiny! They forced the captain and some of the other crew members into a small boat and set them adrift on the ocean. Then the mutineers turned the *Bounty* around and set their course for Tahiti.

Captain Bligh and the others in the small boat made an amazing voyage across thousands of miles of ocean and reached safety. The English navy sent a ship to find the mutineers, and some of them were caught and brought back to England in chains for punishment. But nine of the mutineers had sailed the *Bounty* to a deserted island—Pitcairn Island—to hide from the long arm of English law. There they burned and sank the *Bounty*, so that any ships that might pass would not see it. They began families with their Tahitian wives, who had come to the island with them, and were hidden from the world for almost twenty years. When a ship finally stopped at Pitcairn Island in 1808, only one mutineer was still alive, along with ten Tahitian women and twenty-three children. To this day, the descendants of the mutineers still live on Pitcairn Island.

Captain Bligh was still in his nightclothes when the mutineers took the ship.

The *Victory*

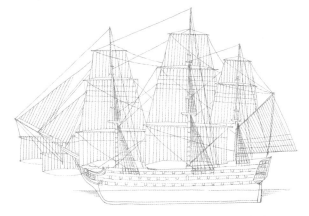

The *Victory* is England's most famous fighting ship, or "man-of-war." It was part of the great "wooden walls of England," the warships whose wooden sides bristled with cannons, protecting the island of England from invaders across the seas. England was the greatest naval power the world had ever known, and with its strength at sea it built an empire around the world.

In the early 1800s the French and Spanish had a large fleet of warships and hoped to invade England. Admiral Horatio Nelson, England's greatest naval hero, sailed the Atlantic Ocean on the *Victory*, searching for the enemy ships. Nelson was legendary in England for his bravery in battle, but he bore the scars of his many victories—his right arm had been cut off, and he was blind in one eye.

In October of 1805, off Cape Trafalgar in Spain, Nelson and his fleet of twenty-seven ships spotted the enemy's thirty-three men-of-war. The enemy ships were lined up one behind the other, with their hundreds of cannons facing the approaching British. But Nelson had a daring plan. Normally enemy fleets would line up opposite each other and fire away with cannons. Nelson surprised the enemy by charging directly into their line. The *Victory* passed, cannons blazing, across the back of the French flagship. *Victory*'s heavy iron cannonballs smashed through the enemy's stern windows and hurtled along the whole length of the ship, smashing everything in their path.

Nelson was directing the battle from the deck of the *Victory*. While his ship was blasting away at another enemy only a few feet away, he was shot down by a musket ball. But when the smoke of battle had cleared, the French and Spanish navies were in shambles. At the end of the day a message was sent from the *Victory* back to England: "We have won a great victory, but we have lost Lord Nelson."

The Victory *was part of the "wooden walls of England."*

The Constitution

In 1797, the United States was a brand-new country with a brand-new navy. One of the first ships built for the U.S. Navy was the *Constitution*, which became the most famous warship in America.

The United States went to war with England in 1812. At that time, the English had the best ships and the best sailors in the world. They thought they would easily defeat the new American navy.

The *Constitution* sailed from Boston and found the British ship *Guerriere* cruising along the coast. For two hours the ships exchanged "broadsides," which means they battered at each other with all of the cannons lined up on the side of the ship facing the enemy. The cannonballs smashed through the wooden hulls, shattered masts, and tore sails and ropes. The relentless broadsides from the *Constitution*'s cannons reduced the *Guerriere* to a helpless hulk, with all three of her masts shot away and her gun decks a wreck. The English surrendered, and the burning *Guerriere* exploded when the fire reached her stores of gunpowder.

During the battle, an American sailor saw that some of the British cannonballs were bouncing off the thick wooden sides of the *Constitution* as if the ship were made of metal. "Hurrah!" he yelled. "Her sides are made of iron!" The *Constitution* had earned her nickname, Old Ironsides.

Twenty-two cannons were lined up on each side of the main gun deck, delivering a deadly "broadside" of iron cannonballs at the enemy.

The Amistad

Forty-nine Africans were chained below deck as the Cuban schooner *Amistad* struggled through a raging tropical storm. Six months earlier, in 1839, they had been kidnapped from their homes in Africa and sold into slavery across the Atlantic Ocean in Cuba. Imprisoned on the dark, wet lower deck of the *Amistad*, one of the Africans, a man named Cinque, managed to break free of the iron collar around his neck. Then he freed the others. The Africans rushed up the ladders, killed the captain and crew, and seized the ship.

The Africans had no experience with sailing, so they left alive the two Cubans on board who had bought them as slaves. They ordered the Cubans to sail the *Amistad* back to Africa. The Cubans, however, only pretended to carry out the orders. During the daytime, they sailed the *Amistad* east toward Africa, but each night they turned the ship around. Eventually, the ocean currents brought them far to the north, and the *Amistad* finally reached land on Long Island, New York. The Africans were captured and sent to a jail in New London, Connecticut, until a court could decide their fate.

The two Cuban slave owners demanded the Africans back as their "property." The government in Cuba wanted them sent back to stand trial for piracy and murder. They were considered to be property, but they were also considered to be thieves—they had stolen themselves! But the judge ruled that they had been enslaved illegally. At that time it was legal to own slaves but it was not legal to capture them from Africa. Only people born as slaves in the Americas could be legally held as slaves. The judge ruled that the *Amistad* Africans should be freed and sent back to Africa.

The case then went to the U.S. Supreme Court. John Quincy Adams, a former president of the United States, defended the Africans. He argued that they had been born free and had a natural right to fight for their freedom. After careful consideration of the legal arguments, the Supreme Court ruled in the Africans' favor. At last they were free! Two and a half years after the revolt aboard the *Amistad*, Cinque and the others finally returned aboard a different ship to their homelands in Africa.

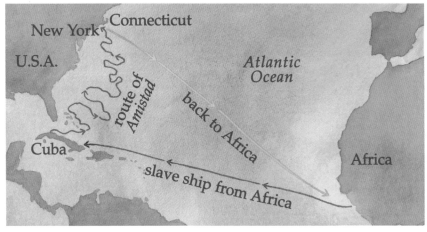

This map shows the journeys of the Amistad *Africans.*

The *Flying Cloud*

The *Flying Cloud* was built for speed. She had a long, graceful hull that sliced through the waves, and with her sails piled high she was faster than any sailing ship the world had ever known. She was a clipper ship, a new breed of sailing ship that raced across the oceans in record time. The clippers were not warships but trading vessels. They dashed around the globe to bring home cargoes such as tea from China or grain from Australia. The fastest ships made the most money for their owners because they could make more voyages and deliver more cargo.

When gold was discovered in California in 1849, a lot of people back East were in a big hurry to go west and strike it rich. The *Flying Cloud* was designed to sail from New York to San Francisco by going all the way around stormy Cape Horn at the southern tip of South America.

The *Flying Cloud* made her first voyage around the Horn in 1851. Her captain, Josiah Creesy, drove his ship and his crew to their limits. Sails tore, masts snapped, and sailors grumbled, but he made it to San Francisco in only eighty-nine days, a record that stood for 138 years.

The age of the great clipper ships was a short one. By the 1860s, more and more ships were built to be powered not by sails but by steam. Steamships were more dependable than sailing ships because they did not rely on the changing winds. The tall ships with their sky-scraping sails were gradually replaced by the chugging, smoking steamers of the modern age.

The harbor of San Francisco was crowded with sailing ships when the Flying Cloud *anchored there in 1851.*

The Monitor & the Virginia

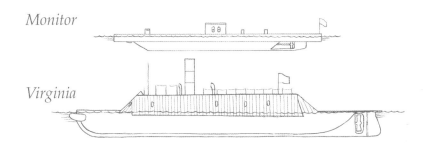

Monitor

Virginia

The battle between the *Monitor* and the *Virginia* changed naval warfare forever. When the Civil War began, warships were still made of wood. They fought by bashing each other with iron cannonballs until one of the ships gave up or was destroyed. But in the early part of the war the Confederates built a brand-new kind of warship called an "ironclad." They refloated the sunken Union ship *Merrimack*, built a structure with iron sides on the deck, put ten cannons in her, and renamed her the *Virginia*. On March 8, 1862, she cruised into the harbor at Hampton Roads, Virginia. Several Union ships were there, and they opened fire on the *Virginia*, but their cannonballs simply bounced off the ironclad's sides. The *Virginia* steamed right up to the Union ships and blasted away. She destroyed two ships before steaming back to port, ready to return the next morning to finish off the rest of the defenseless wooden warships.

But the Union had also been busy building an ironclad. The *Monitor* was a strange and unlikely looking ship. Its iron hull was almost completely under water, and on top of its flat deck it had a rotating turret with two cannons inside. The *Monitor* arrived in the harbor at Hampton Roads several hours after the battle. When the *Virginia* returned the next morning, the *Monitor* was waiting.

The two ironclads fired their cannons at each other for four hours, but neither one was able to damage the other. Both iron ships were completely protected from cannonballs. Neither ship won, but the battle showed that one ironclad would be able to destroy a whole fleet of wooden ships. From then on, all warships would have to be built of iron.

The Monitor *had only two cannons, but that was enough because they were in a rotating iron turret that allowed them to fire in any direction.*

The Maine

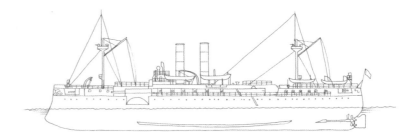

On the evening of February 15, 1898, the United States battleship *Maine* was anchored quietly in the harbor of Havana, Cuba. The captain was in his cabin, writing a letter to his family. Suddenly, he felt a tremendous explosion in the forward part of the ship. Rushing out on deck, he saw that his ship was sinking fast. He scrambled into a rescue boat just as the *Maine* slid beneath the water and settled in the soft mud of the shallow harbor. It all happened so quickly that only 100 of the 350 men on board were saved.

Cuba at that time belonged to Spain. Some Cubans wanted to be independent from Spain, but others did not. The two groups fought each other in violent protests and riots. The United States had sent the *Maine* to Cuba to protect Americans who were there. It was hoped that a mighty American battleship in the harbor might calm things down. But the explosion on the ship caused a crisis.

Some Americans claimed that the Spanish had blown up the *Maine* with an underwater mine. There was no proof of that, but Americans were angry. The slogan "Remember the *Maine*!" was heard throughout the nation, and the United States declared war on Spain. This was the beginning of the Spanish-American War.

Seventy-seven years later, in 1975, the U.S. Navy used modern technology to investigate the cause of the explosion. They concluded that the *Maine* was probably not destroyed by a mine, but by an accidental fire in the coal stored on board the ship.

After the explosion, the Maine *sat in the mud of the shallow harbor for fourteen years.*

The Titanic

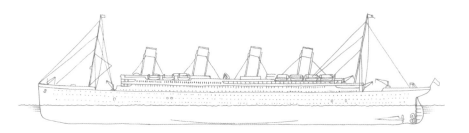

When the *Titanic* was built it was the biggest ship in the world. It was so big that an extra long pier had to be made for its arrival in New York Harbor. But the *Titanic* never reached New York. Its first voyage was also its last.

The *Titanic* left England for a six-day crossing of the Atlantic with twenty-two hundred people on board. The ship made good speed and was hoping to reach New York early. There were reports of icebergs ahead, but the captain did not want to slow down.

The night of Sunday, April 14, 1912, was dark and cold, and no one spotted the iceberg until it was too late. The *Titanic* struck the ice with a glancing blow, but a long hole was opened in the hull and tons of cold seawater began gushing in. Very quickly the captain realized there was no way to save the ship. The front section was filling up with water, which caused the ship to slowly tilt forward. This caused even more water to pour in. He gave the order to abandon ship.

Incredibly, there were only enough lifeboats for about half the people on board. The first few lifeboats that left the ship were not even full, because many passengers were not convinced that the ship was in danger. But as the ship continued to take on water and tilt forward more, people started to panic. When the last lifeboat left, there were still more than fifteen-hundred people on board.

The *Titanic* slid beneath the waves three hours after striking the iceberg. Only 706 people were saved, floating on the cold and empty ocean in the little lifeboats. What began as the first voyage of a proud and mighty ship ended in the most famous disaster in maritime history.

The Titanic *struck the iceberg below the ship's waterline on the right forward part of the hull.*

The *Bismarck*

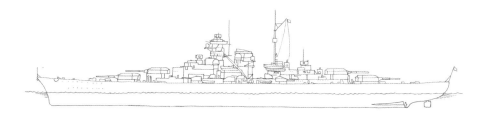

During World War II, the British watched with alarm as their enemies, the Germans, built a huge new battleship, the *Bismarck*. When the *Bismarck* left port on her first voyage in May of 1941, the British set out to hunt her down.

They located the *Bismarck* in the North Atlantic Ocean, and the British navy sent their best battleship, the *Hood*, out to sink the new German ship. The *Hood* was the pride of the British fleet and the symbol of British naval power. When the two warships were about fourteen miles away from each other they opened fire with their powerful, long-range guns. The *Bismarck* was hit and began to leak fuel and take on water. But six minutes later, a good shot from the *Bismarck*'s guns slammed into the *Hood*'s ammunition storage. A huge explosion cut the *Hood* in half, and the British warship sank with over fourteen hundred men on board.

The *Bismarck* steamed away, heading toward German-held waters, and the British began a frantic search for the battleship using forty-eight ships and dozens of planes. After about thirty hours a seaplane finally spotted the *Bismarck*, and British warships and aircraft rushed in for the kill. A group of torpedo planes were the first to get there. Flying through a storm of gunfire from the *Bismarck*, they fired their torpedoes and managed to wreck the ship's steering gear.

Without being able to steer, there was no hope for the proud German ship. British battleships closed in, firing tons of torpedoes and armor-piercing shells. Soon the *Bismarck* was a floating shambles. All her guns were ruined, and she was on fire. A British ship closed in and fired three more torpedoes at close range, and the mighty *Bismarck* rolled over and sank. British ships pulled some survivors from the water, but twenty-two hundred German sailors went down with the ship.

The Bismarck's *captain never gave up. He vowed to go down fighting, and the ship finally sank with her flag still flying.*

The *Nautilus*

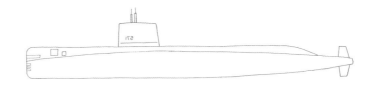

The *Nautilus* was the first nuclear-powered submarine. Before the *Nautilus* was launched in 1954, submarines ran on electric power when cruising underwater and used diesel fuel when on the surface. They were slow, and they could only stay underwater for a few hours at a time. Because the *Nautilus* used nuclear power it was twice as fast as any other submarine and could stay underwater for weeks.

In June of 1958 the *Nautilus* set out from Pearl Harbor, Hawaii, on a top-secret mission to reach the North Pole. There is no land at the North Pole. It is in the middle of the Arctic Ocean, and the water is covered with a huge sheet of ice hundreds of miles across. The captain of the *Nautilus*, William Anderson, steered his sub north toward the Pole, and in the Bering Sea between Russia and Alaska, dove under the Arctic ice sheet. But the bottom of the ice sheet went down so deep that the *Nautilus* was forced to a depth of only a few feet off the seafloor. It was too dangerous, and Captain Anderson had to turn the *Nautilus* back.

The ice sheet melted a little as summer arrived, and the *Nautilus* tried again in July. Captain Anderson was able to find an area where the ice sheet was not too thick. He had plenty of room between the bottom of the ice and the seafloor, but he still had to steer carefully around the huge bottom parts of icebergs that hung down into the sea. At last, on August 3, 1958, at 11:15 P.M., the crew gave a wild cheer as they became the first people ever to travel under the North Pole.

Nuclear power made the Nautilus *the fastest submarine on Earth. The U.S. Navy kept her maximum speed a secret.*

The Enterprise

The *Enterprise* is like a giant moving airport. It carries almost one hundred aircraft that take off and land on a flight deck that's as big as four football fields. It is sometimes called a "floating city" because there are fifty-five hundred people on board along with everything they need to live for months at sea—doctors and dentists, cafeterias and gyms, and even a post office.

When the *Enterprise* was launched in 1960 it was the biggest warship ever built, and it was the first aircraft carrier powered by a nuclear reactor. Because it runs on atomic energy, it sails faster than other ships and much farther. It can go twenty years before it needs to refuel.

The flight deck is huge, but it is not long enough for jets to take off and land the way they do on solid ground. The jets need a little help from the ship. For takeoffs, the flight deck is fitted with four catapults that shoot the jets off the deck at high speed. When landing, a hook on the bottom of the jet catches a steel cable on the ship to stop the speeding aircraft before it reaches the end of the deck. Carrier landings are even more difficult and dangerous in bad weather, when the flight deck is rising and falling with the roll of the sea. Some pilots say that every landing is like a controlled crash.

The nuclear carrier *Enterprise* is the eighth U.S. Navy ship with that name. Since 1775, ships with the name *Enterprise* have symbolized America's strength at sea.

Beneath the flight deck is the huge hangar deck. Half the planes are stored there and are brought up to the flight deck on four giant elevators.

Where Are They Now?

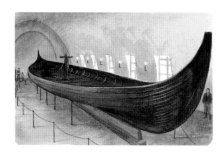

The Gokstad Ship
(pages 4–5)
The Gokstad ship was discovered in a burial mound near Gokstad, Norway. It was dug up, cleaned, and put on display at the Viking Ship Museum in Oslo, Norway.

Cheng Ho's Treasure Ship (pages 6–7)
After the seventh voyage of the treasure fleet, the Chinese emperor outlawed overseas travel and stopped all building and repairs of oceangoing junks. The treasure ships were destroyed.

The *Niña*, the *Pinta*, & the *Santa Maria* (pages 8–9)
The *Santa Maria* ran aground and broke up on a reef off what is now Haiti. The wreck has not been found. The *Niña* was Columbus's favorite of the three ships, and he used it on two more voyages to the New World. No one knows what happened to the *Niña* or the *Pinta* after Columbus's voyages.

The *Golden Hind* (pages 10–11)
The *Golden Hind* was broken up in 1662 because most of her wood was rotten. But to this day there is a chair in the Bodleian Library in Oxford, England, that is made of timbers from the *Golden Hind*.

The *Mayflower* (pages 12–13)
No one is sure what happened to the *Mayflower*. She probably was used as a merchant ship until she got too old and was scrapped. It is rumored that her timbers were built into a barn in Buckinghamshire, England. A replica of the ship, the *Mayflower II*, was sailed from England to America in 1957 and is now docked at Plymouth, Massachusetts.

The *Queen Anne's Revenge* (pages 14–15)
As this book is being written, a team of divers is exploring what they think may be the wreck of the *Queen Anne's Revenge* in Beaufort Inlet on the Outer Banks of North Carolina. A few artifacts from the wreck are on display at the North Carolina Maritime Museum in Beaufort, North Carolina.

The *Bounty* (pages 16–17)
The mutineers burned the *Bounty* and sank it in the shallow harbor of Pitcairn Island in 1790, where it sits to this day. In 1998, a group of divers went to the island and explored the wreck.

The *Victory* (pages 18–19)

The *Victory* has been maintained over the years and is still a part of the Royal Navy of England. It is a popular tourist attraction in Portsmouth, England.

The *Constitution* (pages 20–21)

In 1830 the Navy planned to demolish the aging and damaged *Constitution*. When people protested to save this symbol of American pride, the Navy changed its mind. The *Constitution* was preserved and is still a part of the U.S. Navy. It can be visited in Boston, Massachusetts.

The *Amistad* (pages 22–23)

The *Amistad* was sold by the court in Connecticut for $245. She sailed with a cargo of fruits and vegetables to the Caribbean where she was sold again. There is no record of what happened to her after that. A replica of the *Amistad* was built in 2000 at Mystic Seaport in Connecticut and is sailed for educational purposes.

The *Flying Cloud* (pages 24–25)

In 1874 the *Flying Cloud* ran aground off the coast of New Brunswick, Canada, and broke in two. The wreckage was later burned.

The *Monitor* & the *Virginia* (pages 26–27)

The *Monitor* sank in a storm in the Atlantic Ocean, sixteen miles off Cape Hatteras, North Carolina, in 1862. The wreckage was found in 1973, and some artifacts from the wreck can be seen at The Mariners' Museum in Newport News, Virginia. In 1862 the *Virginia* was burned and sunk in the Elizabeth River near Norfolk, Virginia, by her own sailors to prevent the approaching Union forces from capturing it. Soon after that, parts of the wreckage were salvaged and are in various museums today.

The *Maine* (pages 28–29)

In 1912 the U.S. Army brought the *Maine* up from the bottom of the harbor in Havana. The wreckage was towed four miles out to sea and resunk.

The *Titanic* (pages 30–31)

In 1986 the wreck of the *Titanic* was discovered and explored twelve thousand feet below the surface of the North Atlantic Ocean by a team headed by undersea explorer Robert Ballard.

The *Bismarck* (pages 32–33)

In 1989 Robert Ballard's team found and explored the wreck of the *Bismarck* where it sits at the bottom of the North Atlantic Ocean.

The *Nautilus* (pages 34–35)

The *Nautilus* has been preserved and can be visited at the Submarine Force Museum in Groton, Connecticut.

The *Enterprise* (pages 36–37)

The *Enterprise* is still cruising the oceans of the world.

This book is dedicated to my mother and father.
I owe it all to them.

Special thanks to William Peterson, Senior Curator of
Mystic Seaport: The Museum of America and the Sea
in Mystic, Connecticut.

First published in the United States of America in 2001 by
Walker Publishing Company, Inc.

Published simultaneously in Canada by Fitzhenry and Whiteside, Markham, Ontario L3R 4T8

Library of Congress Cataloging-in-Publication Data

O'Brien, Patrick, 1960-
The great ships / Patrick O'Brien.
p. cm.
ISBN 0-8027-8774-6 -- ISBN 0-8027-8775-4
1. Ships--Juvenile literature. [1. Ships.] I. Title.

VM150.O25 2001
387.2--dc21

2001017873

The artist used watercolor and gouache on paper to create
the illustrations for this book.

Book design by Patrick O'Brien

Printed in Hong Kong

2 4 6 8 10 9 7 5 3 1